Farawaystan

Petter Lindgren

Translated by Lars Ahlström

MARICK PRESS

Library of Congress Cataloguing in Publication Data

Lindgren, Petter
Farawaystan

ISBN 978-1934851-14-2

Copyright © by Petter Lindgren, 2009
Translated from the Swedish by Lars Ahlström
Edited by Ilya Kaminsky
Design and typesetting by Sean Tai
Cover design by Sean Tai
Author photo of Petter Lindgren by Ann Charlotte Ridderstolpe
Cover Art: József Walczak, *Thanatos*, 1998, oil on canvas

Printed and bound in the United States

Marick Press
P.O. Box 36253
Grosse Pointe Farms
Michigan 48236
www.marickpress.com

Mariela Griffor, Publisher

Distributed by
Small Press Distribution
and
Wayne State University Press

FARAWAYSTAN

ACKNOWLEDGMENTS

Grateful acknowledgements to the publisher of ARS Interpres, Alexander Deriev, for his generous advice and support in bringing this book to fruition. This book was made possible to a collaboration between Ars Interpres and Marick Press.

Petter Lindgren Poems Collected from: *Långtbortistan*
   Farawaystan 1994
Porträtt av en död småbåtsägare; *Portrait of the dead owner of a*
   small boat 1997
Ett trögare bläck; *A slower kind of ink* 2000
Landskapet; *The Landscape* 2005

Thanks to the following presses and magazines for prior publications:

Verse The Prose Issue II, Volume 20, Numbers 2&3 2004
   Klondike
   Hydrolysis

Ars Interpress
   Two Skies
   4/5, 2005
   Klondike
   The Fuehrer Alive
   Hydrolysis
   A Slower Kind of Ink

1: SURFACE WATER

the blue nights of April
around the church towers

you dissolve
effervescent gangs of shrill jackdaws

and they bring you back

2: MONOPOLY

You lived in a house that was green
you bought yourself a table of glass
around it you sat making rings and
playing games
It was when the almond trees are in bloom
The stubble on the architects chin was sharper
than the end of a pair of compasses
You tongue taste of gin
He lived in one of the more expensive areas
and you cried hard and openly when he had to
mortgage the yellow streets
and also a blue one with a star on

cried still but a bit less bitter
as he wrote his name on each one of the cards
and buzzingly played that they where floppy disks
that softly slipped in and disappeared
between your ribs
you moved in together
and it did get cheaper that way

To live cramped in a house painted green
on one of the less interesting streets
One of the red ones decorated
with something that looks like soap bubbles
And of course it all buggered up
The iron and the frying pan where stuck at the pawn shop
while the architect went out on the town
A far too obtrusive projectile
in a far too distant war
ripped the arms of a screaming uncle
The shoe rotted and the dog got syphilis

But you photographed well
No one can deny that
The city-street pageant in front of the mirror
And by the table the architect crouched
over his crossword puzzle looking for a synonym
to the word concubine with nine letters
beginning with an m and ending with an s
And it may be right what you say
That the greater part of you has forgotten him.

but not all of you
As sometimes in the morning as you
make your hair into a long and painful plait
and the smell of blueprints and
almond flowers comes to you as a draught
from your pale and in some way
conserved skin on the forearm

3: BALLAD OF A TEEN-AGE QUEEN 5.16

Not so strange

when you have the photo lab
on the bathroom floor

mirjam

that small hairs
end up on the paper

i mean

and leave marks
white scratches

not so bloody

strange when you
take pictures all over the apartment

that the contact print
looks like an entire block of flats

mirjam

with one gable
shoot to pieces

you can be seen standing
in one of the bathrooms

shawing your legs

not so strange
mirjam

that small hairs

4: ENSKEDE

there lies a sorrow in the windows of the house

a forgetfulness I can't remember now

an aeroplane above the roof and the light

that curls like strings of silver

over severed twigs and wings

5: TO A PHOTOGRAPH

Stop! We are
going out here.
Can you see, there
are openings
in the vegetation,
can you see that?
There, they thicken
into a flicker.
There, there is the wind
in the leaves. So,
you have already gone:

6: POPULAR MECHANICS

Nathan is light moulded in the sleep and dragged up.
Dagny is a word that come walking at the bottom of
the piece with a box. Dagny is the sister of Nathan
and her trousers are pink, like poorly fixated photographs.
"What beautiful berries," says Dagny with a voice far
beyond Time of Day. "What beautiful..." And Nathan bent
over the honeysucle, copying his hedge shears:
"Ach Schwester! Ach Schwester!" From the drawers in the
guest-room a fume of death and masonite hits you.

7: ÖRSKÄR NO INFORMATION

        We where transported through summer
and the entire world sat in wicker chairs

Brownish, washed over by reflexes from leaves, from leaves
The road signs did have a warmer colour

another tone of voice

and the mailboxes along the road side bore inscriptions
which revealed that we travelled through a land of old people:

Nilsson 79, Johansson 87, Persephone 81

Somewhere someone is travelling furiously towards you,
at an incredible speed, travelling day and night...

        We where transported through summer
and I remember the veranda where city and country side

have breed into a squeaking hammock

I remember a Nathan and a Dagny
serving apple juice

mixed with one part sorrow and three parts forgetfulness

"– Urin! It's urin!"

   Yes we travelled through summer
and language had not yet learned to fly

was neither high nor low

Farawaystan

hardly a bush and definitely not a tre
no

could neither be hung with stripes
of blue tinfoil

day, Tag –e, m

        The world was a grammar (book)
on the laugh of the thieving magpie
        and a swirl
of silver spoons towards the bottom of the lake

A full dozen

        We where transported through summer
in hired buses with glowing hot seats of red vinyl

We where transported along streams

and in the glimmering between trunks amber coloured creatures
where swimming in water brown like hummus, and some others

incredibly pale

where lying with their bellies against the warm wood of a jetty
counting heads in the water

Big A little A bouncing B,
the system might have got you but it won't get me

One two three four–

The Johnson family travelling in Småland
in a mustard yellow Opel Kadett with registration number –

please call grandma, call grandma

(Rye sandwiches, badminton rackets etc)

        We where transported through summer
and the world was a drained treble-range

at the water's edge

Halftone dots, ladybugs
        "– Lindgren, Lindgren…"

        We where transported through summer
and the world reeled drunk on slowness and glisten
between voices on the beaches

*

Something sank into the skin on the face and remained there
like a remnant

splashing at the edge of the water, fighting

Sleep was never very far away

But will he know where to find you, recognize you
When he sees you, give you the thing he has for you?

8: A HOLOGRAM

In the evening I turn on the light in my globe.
The Pacific Ocean is a big void, so it is facing the wall. No one lives in the Pacific Ocean any way.
Some of the countries on my globe don't exist any longer.
If I go out before dusk, I turn on the light in my globe when I go so that it brightens up the room when I return, especially when I know that I will have company.
Sometimes I go out into the yard to see it glow from there. I'm thinking that it would be strange if I saw myself moving around in the apartment.
One time a woman came back home with me. She immediately turned on the light in the ceiling, that otherwise is only on when I'm fiddle with small tools.
One should be careful to avoid letting out the ugly.
My globe stands on the radio. The light from oceans and continents are reflected in the polished tree and looks like an aquarium.
In the midriff of the radio there is a grey-green magical eye that shows if the station is correctly tuned.
Many cities in the band of frequencies have changed names.
I want people to appreciate both the beautiful music from the radio and the beautiful light from the globe.
"The music is beautiful," I say to people.
And to her that let the ugly out:
"You are beautiful too. Turn of the light in the ceiling!"
Sometimes I listen to weather forecasts for sea area.
Under a lid on the top of the radio there is a gramophone. It doesn't work any longer, but inside it there is a nice light. Just below the lamp is my camera.
When I fold out the bellow of my camera people say:
"Are there still such cameras?"
I have them stand by the radio. I don't use a flash. The exposure time is long. The light falls aslant from below, on the globe the maps have

fallen of in some places.

The glass shows, white like a glacier.

One time I took a picture of the beautiful woman, but she didn't stand still. She kept talking and swinging her long black hair.

The only sharp things in the photograph are the globe and the radio. I don't remember what she looked like.

In spring soundless projectiles fly high above the city. They glitter in the sun like silver coloured dragonflies. No one knows what far away artillery fired them or where they are going. And it's not really my business.

— 2 —

PORTRAIT OF THE DEAD OWNER OF A SMALL BOAT

1: WITH EYES SENSITIVE TO GREEN

1
Dawn rose
like a blue ribbon of light
over the tram rails in the suburb,
writes the French author
Julien Gracq
Who I don't usually read.
But I like that sentence:
Dawn rose
like a blue ribbon of light
over the tram rails in the suburb,
it's a good sentence.
Now I brought out that book again.
I don't know what to do with it.

2
XLII
low tide

In one of the films
from the summer when the Americans
for the first time
landed on the surface of the moon
you can see the two sisters by the lake
wet hair
and the towels left to dry
on the berthing line to the boat

and I don't know
if it's the camera
or the projector

perhaps something to do with time passing
but you can also see something strange
like a dim flicker
like wings on insects
it looks like the world has turned snow-blind

drops fall from the hair of the sisters
sparkling
one of them
pour something that looks like tea
from a thermos
arms reflected in the shiny metal
and it seems to be something funny on the radio
the eyes of the sisters shine

the sea acorns in the grey stone caisson shine.

3
XLI
albedo
The photographer puts his camera aslant, and by mistake lets
the strap dangle in front of the lens, like this, back and
forth, moves slowly back towards land (with his back
towards the rubble stone beach). Then everything begins to shake,
the film comes of the reel. The veil cracks.

4
XL
public road
The public road ends here: in the innermost of July, with a store
and some people, sparrows, flung out under a sky without any sign
of photographic silver. A bit further, in front of a cluster of lilacs
that reveal the presence of a wind, there is a solitary woman in her

sixties: Dagny. I have the impression that she looks straight into the camera, but she doesn't. Under the magnifying glass she just stands there: "Dagny", a wind catcher of thought, a tone, an ice cream sign in the gravel. Further in, among the leaves of the lilac, the graininess becomes too apparent. Space begins, the universe.

5
XXXVII
protection area
The underworld is a grove with old rotted oaks. Our feet sink in the swampy soil and we giggle as the damp trickles between the toes in the sneakers. A bit further there is a bunch of horse carcasses, snorting and pawing in the evening mist. I don't see them at first, almost gets frightened and climbs an almost fallen tree with you close behind. Up there is a small shelf and we stand there a while, trying to figure out if the horses are dangerous or not. Through the weak noise from the highway there is a distant booming filled with something that is similar to the brittle tick of your watch. InterCity train, you say. Your cheeks are shining white in the dark and are so cold. You put your hands on my chest, push me away and look me in the face, says that can't we do something. And we do, we go down from the tree, lay down on the wings you spread on the dewy grass.

6
And for the driver of the train
with his thermos
On his way to Borlänge
at a speed
that is just a fraction
slower than the sunset:
Two orange lights that
driven by a common
more swiftly working relay,

from their round, triangularly
organised orifices
spews out:
The fires of Hell! The fires of Hell!
on each side of the track.

7
XXXV
paternal grand mother
The dark water is not very cold but the rocks on the bottom make it difficult to wade out without falling and get dipped too quickly. When the water goes up to our thighs I can hear
> voices overhead, look up and see a white masthead light wave high up in the sky. I stand just beside the large shiny hull of motorboat that slowly billows in towards the shore. For a few seconds I put my hand against the portside light and the hot glare runs like red soup between my fingers.

8
XXXI
modern war fare
Like my ancestors, their faces in the circle under the dusty, insect-powdered 25-watt lamp the filament can still be seen shining with a remarkable sharpness. As they during the long winter evenings attended to the warts on their feet with the ingredients for gun cotton, that is cotton wads immersed in sulphuric acid. As if there where such a link, as if they, my ancestors, should have had anything to do with the use of land mines in modern war fare. I can't see it in any other way.

9
XXVII
dawn
Smelling bands of rain through the web of the mosquito net.
The movements of the blind are light as fantasies about death.

10
XXIV
I am things made by tortoise
the oval frame and the comb
all like something from fish
Stifled and still longing
the memory of a dark shadow in the seaweed

11
XIX
helen & marion in redwood city
The photograph, taken by grandpa in the US sometime in the twenties, depicts (a) Helen, a child, and (b) Marion, a young woman. Helen and Marion are standing in front of an apple tree in bloom and Marion's arm is somewhat blurred, since she is either (a) on her way to or (b) trying to look like she is on her way to pick one of those small and fair flowers. During the journey to the US my grandpa, who was born and grew up on Torö in the parish of Sorunda, Södermanland, had to pass Slussen in Stockholm. As he later on returned to marry, not with (a) Marion, but another woman (b) my grandma, he passed Slussen again. Most of those who passed the lock during this period in time (let us say five years) belongs to what used to be called The Majority of the Dead. So does also (a) grandpa and probably also (b) Marion, But perhaps not (c) Helen, even though neither she nor Marion ever passed Slussen in Stockholm. The majority of people on earth (and now I mean both (a) the living and (b) the dead) never passed Slussen in Stockholm.

12
XIV
speaker
He died on international water,
without a word in a bed of chromium-plated steel
After having been anchored up in the Com-bay
together with some down hill skiers.

13
XII
Others say
That he enlisted
on one of those old torpedo boats
that run anglers out to the End of the World –
the small outer islet that
the National Administration of Shipping and Navigation has
    chosen to give that name,
since it is a place where no human can be:

The End of the World
No Anchoring

As a warning a black pyramid buoy has been shipped out
after which the travellers are drained of all substance.
Like when a codfish is hooked on a pilk:
and comes whirling in a cloud of its own
                              excrements.

14
V
notes on dead sports men

1
I see the living play soccer on blue grass,
the visiting team in faded orange.
The shirts can't quite keep up.

2
Charlamov died young.

― 3 ―

A SLOWER KIND OF INK

1
THE SPORTS FIELD

You are not supposed to run your bicycle over this sports field
but it's a shorter way home if you do
In the dark it feels almost like in a dream
nothing could happen if you fall
I usually take aim on one of the neon signs on the other side

One by one the aeroplanes pass over the sports field
on their way to Helsinki or Lappeenranta
With fixed and flashing lights

I usually think
while I ride my bicycle over the sports field
about how the airhostesses walk about on high heels up there

Right now
I think
one of them pushes a cart of shining metal
The centre of gravity moves along the body of the airplane

but the change is not significant enough
to be seen on any of the pilots instruments
She can calmly roll along through the aisle
that smell of pirozhki
hard boiled eggs

But then it comes to a halt
One of the other hostesses is in the way
She is leaning in over a seat
in one of those almost obscene postures

Anyway one of the passengers sits
across the aisle
and look at her like this

from behind
as she attempts to push a too voluminous bag
into the overhead locker
It results in some kind of joke

In spite of the fact that both the hostesses are very strictly dressed
in Finnish colours
in blue and white
both begin to laugh

While riding my bicycle over the sports field
I think
If one is to die
one may very well do it in the company of women like these
It is actually a quite comforting thought

And if this passenger
had been turned towards the window
he or she would not
have had so much else to look at

than his or her own reflection
and
with some adjustment of focus

the position light
that encapsulated in the wing seems to shine
with an almost human confidence out there

or at least with a confidence similar to mine
as I now
without light
run my bicycle towards home over this frozen sports field

Shreds of clouds
there is not much else to see
Of my city nothing
Of the industries on the other side of the sports field nothing
If the aeroplane suddenly turns to one side
in that somewhat ominous way
to change direction or commence an approach
possibly a few sparsely lit streets

scattered lights

but other then that only a great empty darkness
that could be any darkness
if only I had not
been riding my bike in it

2
KLONDIKE

At the end of the small tube that the doctor inserts into
the rectum of the patient there is among many other things
a tiny lens and an even tinier light. But there is also a photographer,
a grip, an electrician, a few extras and a recently graduated
script girl from Stockholm. Around this activity a small society
has been created: barracks, day care, a supermarket, a restaurant.
This creates new work opportunities. Some people say that the entire
region has gained new life.

3
THE FUEHRER ALIVE

In the homes of the old people

in the very
old peoples places

the indoor temperature
is always a few degrees above normal

The radio
is turned up louder than normal

you speak louder yourself

On the other hand it's difficult to make yourself understood
It's like skiing in midday thaw

you slide backwards
not forwards

The things you say
are straightforward
almost obscenely honest things

as if wearing far too warm clothes

You hear yourself agreeing that insanity
and artistic skill is something you inherit
or that the people who run the radio station ought to be fired

How your voice ring in the old
peoples ears
it if rings at all

nobody knows

But when the old people sleep

you can move around
in their apartments
quite undisturbed

You get an opportunity to read the serious news-papers
or you can leaf through photo albums
the old people has seen
the Fuehrer
when he was alive

It's quite all right to open the door to the balcony
and get some air

There are titbits in abundance

A look into the bedroom:

The bed lamp is lit
alone in the lull
between two breaths

The cane lies on the bedspread ready for travel

In the kitchen it is peaceful
The white goods shines

But the drinking glasses on the shelf are scratched and ugly
The dishwasher humming under the sink
is responsible for this

The old people
are dishwasher manufacturer's best friends

While the old people are sleeping

you can also take the opportunity to
arrange their pills

These are kept in boxes with transparent lids
sorted after time and day
Wednesday morning

there are two white ones
and a globular blue and yellow one

Actually that box looks like
a block of flats with no roof

There the pills live
almost the same way as the old people

And it is always

some poor lonely
little pill left

when the week comes to an end

4
A SLOWER KIND OF INK

People gather in the squares, point towards the comet which by now has broken through the horizon for the first time in hundreds of years: a small inverted point of rubbed out ink over rooftops in the distance.

5
STRATEGY AGAINST THE COLD

On a morning when the smoke
stood like pink cotton
from the heating company

Just relax
and walk like this
he said

and he began to walk slowly
through the frosty fog on the school yard

like in weightlessness
and with his arms
askew from his body

as if it was of greatest importance
not to oppose
the natural form of
the bulging Stratos jacket
Just relax
he said
and you won't feel a thing

And over the regional hospital
the sun rose
like a swollen red ball

6
SOUTHWARDS, A RAILWAY CROSSING

Soon it will come
But not yet
The light I flashing white
The glass covering the reflectors is ribbed
A thick
and probably impact resistant glass
What else?

There used to be gates instead of bars
Those days
have passed
and shall never come again
The clouds that then passed over the landscape
are now peeling off in the city's art museum
Around the old gateposts poppies grow

Now it comes
A great murmur
like from grasshoppers
A bell can be heard
The little hammer bangs desperately
against the edge of the sounding bowl
The bars lower themselves towards the ground

Even inside the train the bell can be heard
It passes with a sound
that is easy to imitate
but difficult to describe
A resounding meteorite
Someone says:
"How far gone summer is!"

7
HYDROLYSIS

In the cold meat of winter fruit, where cloudbursts move along like
transparent layers, there is a tinge of your hair: shampoo
and poorly impregnated nylon, pollen, stalks
and other green things tangled in the black.
Here and there a taste of zinc, like old mailboxes.

— 4 —

THE LANDSCAPE

1

The lilacs has been thundering (making thunder) this morning
One lies awake thinking
White is far away
has soon forgotten that I existed
*

I guess the leaves have no meaning by them selves
but thunder in all the leaves at the same time
That can't even make a phone call
That the leg gets so big and swollen towards the evening
*

Then the rain have had white
at least here in the house
All the water heater leaking and need to be replaced
roof and beams straightened, ooh!
*

Feels sad to be around your house
when no one is home
White is so long ago
The songs of childhood summers has died away
*

Going to the newsstand
is reminiscent of the lilacs
That one in the middle of the thunder
imagines buying from the lilacs
*

The gravel on the edges
The straight lines
What white got where fragments
The lilacs illuminated
*

Nothing bad in the lilacs!
The lilacs is my life passing
The gasified leaves
The smell of nitrogen
*

Tel. 410 03 that is jangling on the table

White hullabaloo on Klintemo!

The blotting paper gets a vacation
*

The cheek of the thunder has healed now
A White cut
about three centimetres long
A small mark will probably remain
*

Then comes cold air
to put underneath warm
The fabric of the thunder is almost erased
*

After all the rain that fell
white is here
and maybe also in other places
Will go and mail the lilacs here soon
*

Lilacs
the only thing there where without windows
Safes can sometimes be made out of paper
Hey!

2
THE MOTIF

Before the windswept coast
where the pines crawl around
in the lingonberry thickets with their anguish
the waves rise in strict attention
For a brief moment
they strike open their bottle green windows
against the rocks
and the compliant seaweed
But the tormented pines on the beach
neither bows
nor straightens themselves
They just crawl around
with eyes screwed up in the lingonberry thicket
thinking about their anguish

3
GRANDMA VERSUS THE MOON

Grandma is sitting at the other side of the table
soaking biscuits in cold coffee
She stirs slowly with the spoon in the cup
clink clink
the moon comes out over a hillock
The moon haven't got any green checked apron on
the pine forest don't suit grandma
no
but they look quite a lot alike
Both have marks of age on the forehead
Rough areas with a deeper colour
It doesn't look very nice
but it is in a way anyway
Or neither nice or unpleasant at all
Grandma and the moon are beyond such things

4
THE BIG DIPPER

Shines over the landscape
The landscape is getting dusky
Can the Big Dipper read these doodles?

5
THE WAVES

The first wave, sent out by order from the *supreme commander*, rolls in and breaks against shore. *Such white foaming moustaches!*
The second wave, sent out by order of the *head of the marine*, rolls in and breaks against shore. *Such a storm-grey oilskin coat!*
The third wave, sent out by order from the *inspector of minesweepers*, we know him, wasn't he the one who ran a minesweeper aground and had to resign!, rolls in and breaks against the shore.
The fourth wave, sent by order from the commander of the costal navy, rolls in and breaks against the shore. Such stale bilge-water!
Also the fifth wave, sent by order from the *head of the coast artillery*, rolls in and, *ho!*, breaks against the shore, as all the others.
While the sixth (sent by order from the *head of submarines*) instead levels away and collapses in the wake of the fifth: a foaming glass green floor, a *nothing!*
Another wave, number seven, sent by order from the *administration of the marine* and it is actually three in one, three waves huddled up on each others shoulders, sent by order from the *senior physician of the marine, the chief administrator of the marine*
and also the *head of the commissariat corps*, rolls in and, *now damn it!*, breaks against the shore.

Such a mighty tail-heavy roar!

BOOKS BY MARICK PRESS

The Dropped Hand by Terry Blackhawk. ISBN 978-0-9779703-3-9
Never Night by Derick Burleson. ISBN 0-9779703-5-3
Emily Ate the Wind by Peter Conners. ISBN 978-0-9712676-4-0
 (Hardcover); ISBN 978-0-9779703-9-1 (Paperback)
The Blue City by Sean Thomas Dougherty. ISBN: 0-9779703-5-3
American Prophet by Robert Fanning. ISBN-13 978-1-934851-01-2
The Seed Thieves by Robert Fanning. ISBN 0-9779703-0-2
Storm by Katie Ford. ISBN 978-0-9712676-8-8
White Holes by James Hart III. ISBN 0-9779703-1-0
Folding A River by Kawita Kandpal. ISBN-13 978-0-9712676-3-4
The Fortunate Islands by Susan Kelly-DeWitt.
 ISBN 978-0-9712676-6-4
Been and Gone by Julian Kornhauser. Translated by Piotr Florczyk.
 ISBN-13 978-1-934851-05-0
The Boy Who Killed Caterpillars by Joshua Kornreich.
 ISBN 978-0-9712676-7-1
A Complex Bravery by Robert Lipton. ISBN 0-9712676-1-8
It Might Do Well with Strawberries by David Matlin.
 ISBN-13 978-1-934851-02-9
The Sleeping by Caroline Maun. ISBN 0-9712676-2-6
At the Revelation Restaurant and Other Poems by Alicia Ostriker.
 ISBN-13 978-1-934851-06-7
Solute by Daniel Padilla. ISBN 0-9779703-2-9
The Country of Loneliness by Dawn Paul
As When, In Season by Jim Schley. ISBN 978-1-934851-00-5
Witness of Music by Alexander Suczek. ISBN 0-9779703-8-8
Father, Tell Me I Have Not Aged by Russell Thorburn.
 ISBN 0-9779703-6-1
Homage to Paul Celan by G.C.Waldrep. ISBN 0-9779703-4-5
The Catfish by Franz Wright. ISBN-13 978-0-9712676-9-5
INRI by Raul Zurita. Translated by William Rowe.
 ISBN-13 978-1-934851-04-3

www.ingramcontent.com/pod-product-compliance
Lightning Source LLC
LaVergne TN
LVHW011430080426
835512LV00005B/373